The Disapproval of My Toaster

Seth Brown

A Brief Introduction

These are strange times. Certainly, the pandemic has changed many things about the world. But one thing it has not changed is the importance of poetry, which remains as important as ever, although never in as high a demand as one might expect given its importance. Consequently, I was surprised when Dr. Karunesh Kumar Agarwal contacted me and asked me to publish a poetry book with him.

I know that India has been hit very hard by the pandemic, and saw this book as an opportunity to do a little something. So I asked him, if I waived my royalties, would he be willing to donate half of all profits from this book to COVID relief in India. Graciously, he accepted. Thus, I decided that this book would be a pandemic project. Indeed, all of the poems that follow were written during the pandemic, many of them during April 2020 and April 2021 (America's National Poetry Month).

Which is not to say all of the poems are *about* the pandemic. The titular poem was inspired by a bag of gulab jamun mix, and other topics range from spiders to politics to love. But because all of these poems were written *during* the pandemic, they were necessarily affected by it. We have all been affected by it.

And yet, we must go on. So it remains for me to thank the people who made going on with this book possible. WordXWord, for pushing me to write prolifically every April. Debbie and Michelle, for their constant love and support. Dr. Karunesh Kumar Agarwal, for his kind invitation and ceaseless mission to publish poets and bring their poetry to a global audience. Friends and family too numerous to list. And last but certainly not least, you (yes, you!) for reading this collection of my poems. It is my sincere hope that you enjoy them.

—Seth Brown

RisingPun.com

Contents

"Spider Funeral"

Spiders are the proof
That I'm not a good person
Because I know
I should let them live
And I do,
Whenever I encounter one at my desk
Because I don't want to kill for no reason
But
Whenever I encounter a spider in the shower
Creeping towards my naked body
I kill it
Because I feel vulnerable
But I always feel bad afterwards
Which I hope is a sign
That I'm not an evil person either.

"Pedestrian Problems"

Many people are afraid of public speaking;
I'm afraid of private speaking.
Put me on a stage in front of 50 people
And I can perform for an hour;
Comedy, poetry, or just an improvised rant.
No problem.
But if I have to ask a stranger
For a favor
Hooooooooooooooooooookay.
I will need at least five minutes
To psych myself up
And will feel terrible from the moment the need occurs to me
Until I've managed to successfully ask
Or just as likely
Until I've thought of a plausible alternative
So I can avoid asking.
Five miles
Is the longest distance I've ever walked
To avoid having to ask a stranger for a ride
So far.

"The Scrivener"

"I know it doesn't pay a lot,
But I figured you could help her out
Since you weren't doing anything important."
Exactly.
I wasn't doing anything.
Important!
We've somehow lost sight
Of the value of leisure
Reserving rest as an elite reward
For those who are retired
Or dead.
The Puritanical ideal
Lives on as constant hustle
Where everyone is always on their grind
And announces it proudly.
Grind: Verb.
To crush, pulverize, or reduce to powder.
We still act like nothing is more important
Than to be constantly be doing something.
But I think
Nothing
Is
More important than to constantly be doing something.
Because there's value in having room to breathe
To let your mind wander
And if idle hands and minds are the devil's workshop,
Then have yourself a hell of a time.
Because sometimes not doing anything
Is everything.

"Thieves"

They say when you stay up late,
You're only stealing from your future self
But between debt and climate change
Everyone else is stealing from your future self
So you may as well get there first

"Rara Avis"

I am a night owl
Always awake at 3 am
When my town is asleep.
It has been suggested
I move
From my sleepy Massachusetts town
To the West Coast
The casinos of Las Vegas
Or New York
The city that never sleeps
But who needs night owls there
A tree in the forest may not make a sound
But a tree in the middle of the city is an oasis
Here I shall remain
Where the trees are many
And the night owls are few

"Apparently, Einstein Didn't Flunk Math"

Love is not a transitive property.
I learned this in high school
Not in math class
But when the girl
The one who mattered
Had one boy who mattered
And I hated him
For not being me.

A few decades later,
When a woman I love
Finds someone who makes her happy
He makes me happy too
Which I guess goes to show
You can't believe everything you learned in school.

.

"A Penny Saved"

I would never describe myself
as cheap.
Parsimonious?
Absolutely.
Frugal?
Definitely.
Penurious?
Sure.
Thrifty?
No doubt.

They say when you have a hammer,
everything looks like a nail.
But even when you see an actual nail,
you might try to avoid using a hammer
if you had a 1,000-piece fancy tool set,
Which incidentally
is a thing I would never buy.

"#140 characters"

It's unfair that the space
Counts as a character
Is what I used to think
But self-isolation has convinced me
That space has a character too

"10 Ways I Know I'm Not Okay"

10) I feel adrift, trapped in a parallel dimension, lost in time, and waiting for the Avengers to fix it so I can get back to real life.

9) I've stopped playing my favorite engrossing video games because I no longer have the mental focus to immerse myself.

8) I've begun accepting that this actually is real life.

7) I have to have a great day – no work due, partner bakes me cookies, etc. – to feel as happy as I used to feel on a normal day.

6) Robin Williams asks me if I've been feeling the void lately. I admit that I have, and he tries to give me a pep talk, but I'm consumed with guilt for not being able to do anything for him.

5) I try to read the rules to a boardgame on my shelf and can't make sense of it. I tell myself I'll come back to it later. I try again a few days later, and give up again. Before the pandemic, friends would lend me their new games and ask me to learn the rules so I could teach them. Now I can't even teach myself.

4) I step into a building and realize I've forgotten my mask. Suddenly, tons of people, all maskless, begin flowing through the entrance until I'm trapped in a sea of people.

3) I've started to have a difficult time distinguishing dreams from reality.

2) I am a frog.

1) I've stopped pretending I'm okay.

"Pandemic Regimen"

My parents told me
I should really get in shape.
Well, round is a shape.

"Love In The Time Of Corona"

Long-distance relationships are terrible
But when I want to be with you
Any distance greater than 50 feet
Is a long distance
There is no meaningful distinction
Between five miles away
And five hours away
There is only here
And not here
And yet
You don't have to be here
To have presence here
The thought of you
Warms me through the cold winter's night
Your glow
Incandescent
Lighting up a room
That you're not even in

"Halcyon"

I come from a community
that was a community
Neighbors who were neighborly
because their kids were friends
and they were too
People who all cared
about each other

It's not like that here
but then again
it's not like that there now either
Maybe I imagined the whole thing

"Life Lessons"

As I take a cookie off of the plate,
My uncle tells me to hold it up to the moon
Try to line it up so the top curves match,
But there is a thin border of moon
Around the cookie.
It takes me a few seconds
But then he tells me to focus
On the border between moon and cookie.
I contemplate this border for a few more seconds
And when I look back down
The rest of the cookies are gone
And my uncle is laughing

"Tender Children"

(an ekphrasis on Francisco Goya's masterwork "Saturn Devouring His Son")

Who among us hasn't wanted
to devour their child
Tears and blood
streaming from both of you
But then a blessed quieting
of the fears that you
will be surpassed
No more the worry
of being pushed aside
so the new generation may thrive
Put them back inside you
where they began

"Raising the Bar"

The word Barbarian
Originated in ancient Greece
When the Greeks heard foreigners
Speaking in a foreign language
And rather than having the empathy to say,
"These people probably have a language
And culture worth studying
Just like we do!"
The ancient Greeks said,
"These idiots
Just walk around saying 'Bar Bar Bar'!"
As did the Romans
By which I mean
The Romans used the term barbarian
To apply to all those without Roman culture
But I also mean
That the Romans
Were originally considered barbarians
By the Greeks
So to answer your question
No
I don't think the song was garbage
Just because it's not your type of music

"Measure For Measure"

The distance between me
And the person you wish I was
Is the distance between us
Not because it has to be
But because every time you measure it
I can feel your hands stretch out
And push me away

"I Know Why The Flipped Bird Tweets"

I receive a temporary ban
For telling him,
"Fuck off with that nonsense,"
Because I was rude
Instead of polite like he was
When he suggested not all people are people
And that the people he doesn't think are people
Don't deserve the same rights as people he approves of.
After all, I was just being rude,
And he was offering a discussion,
And this is a forum for digital discussion.
But I say, technically speaking
The middle finger is a digit.

"The Southern Migration"

The fact that men lose their hair
as they get older
is proof God has a sense of humor
And the fact that the hair stays in the rear
is proof that sense of humor is sophomoric

"Chill"

Looking out the window at the playground
Covered in freshly-fallen snow
Pristine and untouched
Five-year-old me couldn't wait to ruin the shit out of it
Vandalizing the backyard with footprints and fall-prints
As if to say
"Fuck you, natural beauty, this is my town!"
I wish everyone else
Had grown out of this too

"The Disapproval Of My Toaster"

Everyone yells at inanimate objects
But I can feel them staring at me.
Not all at once;
I'm not crazy.
I'll just sometimes find myself alone in a room
With a certain object staring at me,
As if to say,
"Hey, what happened to all those plans we made?
We were going to do things together
I'm here because we were going to do things together
And I've kept up my end of the bargain."
Well, I'm sorry, Piano.
I'm sorry, Bag of gulab jamun mix I purchased in 2013.
I wish I could be a better person for you,
But we both know I'm not,
So I've had to move on.
But I want you to know:
I still think about you sometimes.

"Quicksave"

I often wish
that life were like a videogame
with save states I could reload
whenever I made a mistake
But a friend pointed out
that if I had such a power
and used it
I'd still be in third grade.

"Don't Be Cross"

Elvis died on the toilet
And I think if Elvis came back
To find all his biggest fans
Were putting up toilet shrines
And wearing toilet necklaces
The King would be a little confused
And a little upset
But hey it's your life
Wear whatever religious necklace you want

"It's Good To Be The King"

When I was growing up
I wanted to be Mel Brooks,
Who wrote many funny movies
And also funny TV shows,
And hilarious musicals,
And brilliant routines with Carl Reiner,
Pretty much funny everything.

I envisioned the man as
A non-stop creative humor writing powerhouse.

But the other year, I saw a video of his life these days
And the way he spends evenings in old age
Is not furiously writing hilarious scripts,
But getting together with his best friend (Carl Reiner)
So they can eat takeout food from their favorite deli
And watch TV together.

And it made me realize
I still want to be Mel Brooks.

"A Single Kernel"

He said, "I want that one-horned creature, rarest of the beasts!"
So beasts who had one horn showed up, in hopes it was their
day.
"I meant a unicorn; no other creature's worthy in the least!"
And so, the creatures sadly turned around and went away.

The rhino wondered if he was too large to be desired.
The narwhal sobbed and wondered if she might not be too wet.
Were these poor creatures lacking all the noble traits required?
Nope, they simply hadn't met the proper people yet.

Then came a unicorn, in all its alabaster glory!
"At last, my unicorn! Come and be joined with me!", he said.
The unicorn replied, "Narwhal and Rhino shared their story,
So I've decided that I'd rather hang with them instead."

"Pocket Full of Artifice"

Abraham Lincoln told me
that I should buy myself a donut
if I wanted a donut
because I could afford to treat myself
and I was worth it.

The Andrew Jackson Twins told me
that I was a valued and important member of society
whose contributions were recognized
and that I would be accorded respect
and feel accomplished.

A chorus of George Washingtons told me
that everything was going to be fine
because the gears of commerce were still turning
and normalcy would be restored soon.

Presidents are liars
Which is why if you want to know how your life is really going
You need to do some actual introspection
And can't just count the presidents
In your pocket.

"Less Is More"

I write more poetry
when I am depressed
My partner writes more fiction
when life has her stressed
We both find that lately
we've been writing less
And we have agreed
this is for the best

"Revelations"

Context is everything.

A smattering of laughter
Is not the reaction you generally want
When coming out to your parents

But if you happen to be coming out to your parents
Via a series of jokes in your comedy set
Which you are currently performing on stage
A smattering of laughter is nice to hear

On the car ride back
They say they enjoyed your set
And you say you are glad, because it's all true
They do not comprehend, so you explain it again slowly
To their sputtering surprise
They did not understand you meant what you were saying
Because context is everything

"Best Intentions"

A white moustache
Frizzled white hair
And a boyish grin
Pete took the stage
And did what he did
Best
He played the drums
But the most impressive thing
About Pete
Is what he didn't do
Regret
He didn't demean his life
By constantly comparing it
Unfavorably
To the life he could have had
He said,
"I wouldn't change it. I'm happy."
He may not be bigger than Jesus
But he had the equanimity of Buddha
And avoided the snares
He wasn't playing.

"The Canny Valley"

Brave little toasters
Singing candelabras
And pull-string cowboy dolls
Anthropomorphized objects
Capture our hearts
By taking on some human qualities
But not taking on the ugly mess
Of being human

"Terrible Mistake"

calloused hands washing
another thirty dishes
another pile of silverware
calloused hands washing
everything, attached to
a man who knew nothing
but hard work
and a love
for his family

he had made the terrible mistake
of being born
in el salvador
instead of here
but had saved his money
and spent his sweat
and made it to
these golden shores
to find a better life
for his family
which he had found
temporarily
until his asshole co-worker
was fired
and decided to retaliate
against their boss
by calling ICE
who arrested the man
for his terrible mistake

and removed him
and his calloused hands
from our country
to keep it safe
for the kind of people
who destroy a dishwasher's life
yet somehow believe
their hands are clean

"The Money Men"

Clink
Clink
The sound of coins
Is the only thing
They care about
Clink
Clink
It is so clear to me
That it never crosses my mind
To ask if they might care
About saving countless foreign lives
Clink
Clink
But when the world is interconnected
And diseases abroad
Soon become diseases at home
Wouldn't you want to stop it while you can?
Clink
Clink
There is no reply
As the diseases that will one day return
To kill family and friends
Rage on across the seas
Clink
Clink
There is no reply
Save for the sound
Of another 30 pieces of silver
In a pill-maker's pocket
Clink
Clink

"Casual Ties"

Contrary to popular belief
Most soldiers do not want a war
But that's never their call
Any more than the immunocompromised
Can make you get a vaccine and self-isolate
Funny
How the people making decisions resulting in death
Never seem to be the ones doing the dying.

"Daunte Wright"

The verb "wait" does not always take an object.
But the concept of "wait" always anticipates one.
Without an object, you are not waiting;
You are sitting around doing nothing.
If you wait, you must wait **for** something.
So when another young Black man is killed by police
And the people cry out for justice and reform,
You must have an object in order to ask us to wait.
Are we waiting for widespread evidence of police brutality?
For a Democrat in the White House?
For a murder on video?
For more to occur in the same city before the trial for the previous one is over?
Without an object, you literally cannot ask us to wait.
You are only asking us to do nothing,
And we have done enough of that already.

"Chalk Angels"

hard-boiled detectives
investigating the crime scene
chalk outlines
where bodies should be
necessary clues because
nobody knew what happened
until the end of the episode
where they caught the murderers
and put them in prison
these days
everybody knew what happened
sometimes there is even video
but the chalk outlines
are in the prison

"Dead Letter"

All becomes clear.
Death everywhere, from greedy humans.
I just know life means not oppressing people
"Quit resisting!", say the untouchably violent
Weaponized xenophobic young zealots.

"Public Filing, Nestle Corporation"

Water
Belongs to
Everyone
And I'm part of
Everyone
So it belongs to
Me
Thus I can
Take
As much as I want
And if there's none left for
You
Then you can pay
Me
For some of
My
Water

"The New Era"

I thought we had all agreed
It was the dawn of a new era
But   we
Wasn't   all
Not the children still in cages
Not the starving Americans and starving Iranians
Still watching America's budget sent up in planes and dropped as explosions
Not the people still being killed in mass shootings
Or by police
In many ways, it's similar to the old era
But in this new era
I am no longer surprised

"A Trick Of The Light"

optical illusions are amazing
you can look at something concave
and it appears convex
or you can look at someone else
and see only their accomplishments
but then look at yourself
and see only your flaws

"Hope"

I tell her
things could always improve
but a few minutes later
I ask her
could things improve?
because I'm not a doctor
and she's the one
living in constant pain
and I'm the one
desperate to give her
reasons to keep living
and neither of us
want me
to be a liar

"Moving Goalposts"

I realize she's not your kid,
But even after she gets into grad school,
You say she's "not that smart".
And that hurts me.
You don't think she's good enough
For the fancy job she applied for,
And you say I'm biased because I love her,
But maybe I'm not because they hired her,
And you're still acting like she's not good enough.
When she wins the award for her work,
You say it's a fluke, as you do
When she wins another award
Time and again the world provides evidence
That I am right about her
And you don't give her enough credit
I just wish you'd be nicer
To yourself

"UnMarked"

The time my best friend said I had to meet you because we'd hit
it off, and I was unconvinced

The time you made kettle corn for your fellow groomsmen, and I
immediately liked you

The time we played Taboo as a team having just met the previ-
ous day, and kicked the asses of couples who had been together
for ten years

The time you came to visit, and my girlfriend at the time was
rude to you, and I started to fall out of love with her

The time you came to visit at the new house, and brought your
proudest creation, the world's most perfect scratch record

The time I was excited to learn that you were moving to a town
near me, so we could hang out more often

The time I was sad to learn that you had taken your own life
during the move, and had been depressed for months

The time I missed you

The time I wondered if I could have saved you

The time I missed you

"Life of the Party"

Please stay
At least a little longer
You can always leave later
If you decide you're really not enjoying yourself
But I'd love to help you enjoy yourself
Because this party will be much worse
Without you here
Can I get you anything
You're welcome to anything in my fridge
Or maybe there's some music you like
Or we could play a game or something
I don't know
What will convince you to stay
I wish I were a better friend
I wish this were a better party
But it could still get better
Maybe something awesome will happen
And things will really improve
Next year
Could you at least
Stick around until then
You can always leave later
But if you leave now
You'll miss out on everything
And I have lost too many friends already

"The Dark Ages"

that summer i wore
sunglasses all the time
even at night because
i was afraid to let
the light in but then i
got so used to them that
the light hurt
my eyes and made it
harder to give
them up until
years later when i
realized i needed to let
the light
in

"Spirit of St. Louis"

the blur of movement
outside my window
resolves itself
into a cardinal
that alights
on the tree
tiny, yet resplendent
in crimson
standing out
amidst the bare twigs
and browned leaves
at which it glances
with worry
i, too
wish it were spring already

"Night Vision"

She braces herself
For the angry words
That do not arrive
And when instead
He smiles and thanks her
She asks in confusion,
"You're not mad at me
For correcting you?"
And now it is his turn
To ask in confusion,
"Why would I be mad at you
For sharing information with me
When you know more than I do?"
The question hangs in the air
As she stares into space.

When you ask Europeans
What it's like to visit America,
One of the things they usually mention
Is how weird it is
To see American flags
Everywhere.
Do Americans frequently forget
What country they are in
And need helpful reminders?
Other countries do not do this.

Sometimes it's hard to see
That the place you are in
Is not   normal
Until you are no longer there.

"Ladies, Give Your Man What He Likes"

He doesn't like when you are out
and chatting with your friends
He doesn't like your contradictions
of what he defends
He doesn't like the time you spend
with passion to create
He doesn't like the junk you do,
when it's His stuff that's great.
In short, it's very clear:
He doesn't like to be outshone.
So help prevent that terrible state
By leaving him, alone.

"Suffering Sappho"

She wants their endeavor
To be forever.
She tells her, Never forever.
But meanwhile?
Meanwhile.
At first, it tears her up inside,
But then she decides
She could live with meanwhile
Forever

"The Love Drug"

Studies by neuroscientists
using MRI brain-scans
have shown that love
has the same effect on the brain
as a drug

We all know some people
who get high on their own supply
And some
in withdrawal

Some who partake
a little too much
shutting out the rest of the world
to focus on riding the high

I am trying to use responsibly
a couple hits over the course of the day
Not so much that I can't do my work
just enough to give me a slight buzz
all day long

"Envisioning Love"

It's easiest to fall in love
with a blur
Moving too fast to pin down
or just fuzzy around the edges
Avoiding the little details
that bother you
when you stare at a picture too long
You can fall in love
with a vague blurry outline
and your heart fills in the rest
Perhaps that's why
you don't wear your glasses in bed

"Marginalia"

I grew up believing
As most of us did
That the main text was the important thing
And the little scribbles in the margins
Didn't matter
But from a historical perspective
Scholars become most interested in the marginalia
In how they can sometimes tell us more about the author
Than the text itself
I think about this sometimes
When we are both sitting together
Doing nothing important at all

"A Comprehensive List Of Everything I Need During Self-Isolation"

1) Food
2) Internet
3) You

"It's A Shame That Hestia Is One Letter Off From Being An Anagram Of Atheist"

I have watched her making the peanut sauce
At least a dozen times
Plus she told me the recipe
But although I have used the exact same ingredients
I have once again created an unsatisfying imitation
Which I bear in supplication
Simultaneously seeking forgiveness and the blessing of improve-
ment
And I receive both
The only god that ever answered my prayers
Was love